GRACE NOTES

AND OTHER POEMS

ANDY BROWN & MARC WOODWARD

SEA CROW PRESS

AMPLIFYING VOICES

PRAISE FOR THE AUTHORS

Grace Notes

'From the intimacy of a pub singalong or an epiphany in a guitar shop, to virtuosic frenzy or the majesty of a symphony, *Grace Notes* is endlessly inventive, clever and heartfelt. I love this book — it's so friendly and inviting you hardly notice it playing your heartstrings or lighting up your brain like a mixing desk, and before you know it you're part of its score.'

—*Luke Kennard, Winner of the Forward Poetry Prize. Professor of Creative Writing, University of Birmingham.*

Reviews of the authors' other recent work

The Tin Lodes (written collaboratively)

'This is a very fine collection, a closely observed and well-researched piece of work that succeeds in operating on several different levels at once. The collaboration is seamless and a testament to the way these two writers have worked so well together on this project. Fully recommended.'

—*Quill & Parchment*

Of their individual work:

Andy Brown

'A love of language and willingness to play with music, meaning and the reader's expectations and perceptions.'

—*Poetry Review*

'With its love of ideas and language, his work demonstrates that there need be no barriers in poetry; that the philosophical, the lyrical and the playful can be combined in work of assured and generous vision.'

—*John Burnside*

Marc Woodward

'As well as a poet, Woodward is an accomplished musician. His poetry is correspondingly neat, practised, highly lyrical. The poems are singing, in a predominantly minor key, but they are a joy to listen to.'

—*Acumen Literary Journal*

'Beautifully crafted poems...that sing in the dark of darkness.'

—*Canto Magazine*

ACKNOWLEDGMENTS

We gratefully acknowledge the support of the editors of the following magazines and publications where some of these poems, or earlier versions of them, were published:

Acumen Literary Magazine; Allegro Poetry Journal; A Restricted View Under the Hedge; Atrium; The Crank Magazine; Dreich Magazine; Ink, Sweat and Tears; International Times; Open Arts Forum; Poetry and Covid (Plymouth & Nottingham Trent Universities); *Poetry Salzburg; Prole Magazine; Raceme; Stride Magazine,* and *The Trust Territory* (Heaventree Press).

CONTENTS

INTRODUCTION

Poets Andy Brown & Marc Woodward are both musicians, songwriters and performers who have been playing, recording and performing music their whole lives. For nearly ten years they have also written and played music together around the festivals and pubs of South West England. In 2020 they published a collaborative book of poems, *The Tin Lodes* (Indigo Dreams) and, following that, began this new collaboration, *GRACE NOTES*, a book of musical poems.

The poems in *GRACE NOTES* are about musicians, composers, performers, music teachers, and song writers – from Captain Beefheart and Santana, to Elvis and Bowie; from Cole Porter and Dave Brubeck, to Nina Simone and Susan Tedeschi. Other poems relate to sound, music and song in different ways, including poems about instruments, gigs and recordings, as well as several poems about natural sound and environmental change. The collection begins and ends in silence, starting with poems written during the Covid pandemic in 2020, and ending with lullaby and meditation.

In music, a grace note is a brief note that ornaments and embellishes the note that follows it. In that spirit, the poets took inspiration from each other's poems to make *GRACE NOTES* a musical improvisation on – and call-and-response to – each other's writing. Each one of the poems was written by one or other of the poets, but they were all edited, shaped and sequenced collaboratively. In tune with their musical collaborations, the poems are presented here anonymously as the work of the ensemble.

GRACE NOTES

My Instruments Begin to Speak

My instruments begin to speak,
calling softly to each other,
waking the stillness of the room.

Perhaps the changing weather
makes them gently shift and creak,
timber easing, strings letting go,

tension starting to release.
Or are they lamenting music,
unemployed, silent, for so long?

They know nothing of human illness,
the shuttered pubs in villages,
the fate of fragile businesses.

And I have no heart to tune them.
I let the dust rest, shuffling
barefoot through the same few rooms.

The instruments sigh in their sleep.
Hard over the garden's remnants,
this world in limbo, the wind booms.

Hurdy Gurdy Player with Dancing Dog

Cornelis Dusart, etching, 1685

Strange to think that, once, these streets were noisy,
now that Lockdown's brought them to a hush:
the cars are gone, the buses at a standstill
and all those schoolkids – babbling on their way,
hollering from one kerb to the other –
are shut indoors, in silence, with their screens.

The main road at the garden's end has dwindled
to sporadic slipstream air and humming tyres.
No parting aeroplanes drone high above,
and I'm grateful for that at least. Grateful
for the song of birds; the rush of the wind
in the cherry; the swish of birch and ash.

It's like we've gone back to a simpler time,
a calmer age in which I can hear myself
think. I'm so used to the quiet, even
the doorbell makes me jump... I know it's just
the postman delivering the boxes
of things we bought online and don't much need,

but I'm half expecting to open the door
like that old dame in Haarlem, 1685,
to find a hurdy gurdy player there
in the muddled street, a spill of children

trailing in his wake, and a little dog
dancing in a collar and suit, yapping

as he prances on his hind legs. And why not?
Silence is imagination's maker
greeting the music of the possible...
while the vines around her porch continue
to house the pairing woodpigeons who coo
steadily, as if nothing much could change.

Pieter Breughel at the *Augan* Accordion Festival

With dancing from the villagers amassed –
their fingers linked, their feet recounting rings –
Pieter Breughel sits to watch and sketch

a hundred keen accordionists
squeezing the air through their clickety clack
on the stage of the humid village hall.

Nothing much has changed, he supposes.
In the promising girl in her pageant dress
and the headstrong boy who tries too hard

he sees himself and his own girl; in the neat
old man and his rake of a woman he sees
his father *farandoling* with his wife.

Outside, the canal's sluggish vein pulses
through the nearby valley as the memory
of a folk tune comes to him like rain,

as if some August storm was asking
whether he wanted to return or remain;
as though there was a choice.

The warm room and the soft rain...
the century old ceremonies of summer...
most of the time the answer he reaches is *now*.

Ross Hamilton and Marc

Tuesday Nite at the Nevill Crest and Gun,
relaxing background music while you dine:
Cafe Accordionist Ross Hamilton.

Often joined by his busy-fingered son:
'Fastest exponent of the mandoline!'
Thursday Nite at the Nevill Crest and Gun.

Booking essential if you plan to come
and, free with every steak, a glass of wine.
Breton shirt and beret: Ross Hamilton.

He plays a Zerosette Leviathan
complete with built-in strings and drum machine
Sunday Nite at the Nevill Crest and Gun.

Three times a week and special occasions
(Beaujolais Nouveau and St Valentine's)
Oo la la! It's Monsieur Ross Hamilton.

Ross plays all requests, any tune you hum –
no punk or disco, or much post '59,
just 'standards' at the Nevill Crest and Gun.
The great Ross Hamilton – and Marc, his son.

Night Driving

Winding through Ashdown Forest,
coming home late from a gig,
dad driving, me just fifteen,
we scan the skies for U.F.O.s –
streaking with unfeasible speed
or static, lit like bright cigars.

Moths flare and die in our headlights
as we stitch junctions together.
Cottage windows on far ridges
shine with no greater mystery
than the unknown lives of people
existing much the same as we.

Dad tells ghost stories: a shot stag
hung to die in a hotel cellar,
a walled-in child knocking
ceaselessly from a doorless room.
He vows to come back after death
so I'll know, one way or the other.

Forty years later I'm returning,
alone, down moonless lanes
after a 'last respects' visit
to a faint and papery aunt.
I watch the void of heaven
for unexplained illumination.

A low owl flaps across the road.
Still the only lights come from
dark hamlets, nameless in the night
and the windows of roadside inns
as empty as ghost stories,
aliens and unkept promises.

Mister Hielz

The day was divisions and fractions
when Miss T. told us *'Children, stop
what it is you're doing... pay attention.
This is Mister Hielz.'* The sallow stranger
wore a suit that even my grandfather
would have taken to the charity; a hat
I'd seen in some library's history books.

'You, you and you,' he said, mechanically,
picking out his victims in what seemed
a purely random manner. Those of us
who'd had the finger pointed, stood
awkwardly and shuffled through the door,
not knowing where we headed to or why,
feeling *their* eyes on *our* backs as we went.

In the soundless room behind the library
we stared at the reflections in our shoes.
'This...' said Mister Hielz, *'is Mister Violin
and you will follow and obey him well.
He'll be a friend for life if you work hard,'*
his foreign vowels and consonants
meaning we only half heard him...

and only half understood *what* we heard
as he slathered the horse-hair with rosin,
shouldered the rosewood and conjured
a Slavic reel that held us mesmerised,
and keeps us spellbound decades on,
in the preparatory tuning up of orchestras;
the ghostly loops of fiddles in subways.

Viola Da Gamba Lesson

Viola perches like a waisted owl,
pretty in her tawny wood and purfling.
Tentatively I try to make her sing –
she answers me with screeches, hoots and howls.

Like a falconer, I hood and starve her.
In the dark she creaks, untested, patient.
Finally when I think she might relent
I bow before her, begin the torture.

With rosined tail hair from Russian ponies
I carefully approach her underhand
and stroke her in a way she might withstand
to no success – she merely squeaks at me:

'I'm not some easy strummable guitar:
I'm your mistress – learn here how flawed *you* are.'

A Music Teacher Takes Science Class

The teacher chalked an outline of a brain
upon the board. *Today we'll think about*
how music works, how 'earworms' operate.
He squiggled curly shapes across the sketch.
These lines are channels – canals you might say –
and indeed if you imagined Venice
you wouldn't be a million miles away.
From these canals melody floods the brain,
like the lagoon through Cannaregio
and under the screened-off gallery
of the Ospedale Della Pieta
where, once, Vivaldi's cloistered virgins
bowed his high baroque for wealthy merchants –
    but I digress.
               On an atomic scale...
he drew a circle with a central dot
...an atom with its nucleus in place...
then drafted several oval orbits
...and here we have the bright electrons,
each revolving round that tiny hub –
and this pure emptiness in which they whizz,
the unfilled void in every cell of us,
is, I believe, the house where music lives.

Mandolin in Barham House

Mike is thumping out Joplin in room three –
'The Entertainer' and 'Maple Leaf Rag'.
Upstairs a violin resists the bow
while somewhere down the hall a clarinet
is falling off the ladder of its scales.
Free periods can be spent in practice,
disturbing the dust motes above the big
radiators, lifting them to polka
in beams from the high Victorian windows.
I shouldn't be here though – I have no grade
exams to study for, no grand solo
or orchestral part in the next school show,
but my enthusiasm wins a pass
and Mr Williams doesn't seem to mind
although, today, he stops me in the hall:
Isn't it high time we put your talents
to the violin, not that folk-tune toy?

Holding the Beat

My brother played a kit but never showed me
how to paradiddle or tap the ride;

that was left instead to trial and error
and the maddened instruction of friends:

When you can pat your head and rub your belly
at the same time, you'll get it. Now, let me...

I never could and, still, can only play
one basic rhythm: the learner's stomp

against the kick drum, counting one and three,
with the snare coming in on the backbeat,

or the simple slap and brush of a *cajón*
as I pit-pat at the back of the stage

and try to give the moment – and my past –
a backbone firm enough on which to build.

Humber Drums

Drum beats echo from the Iron Age fort at Humber
    Down
carried on the same wind bringing fieldfares from the
    north.

The oxen are tethered, old ceremonies have begun –
until the drums and chants are drowned out by a
    London train

pushing time and air away along the further bank
though close enough to see a passenger with headphones

nodding to his secret beat. The train curves out of sight
to where the ocean spills its souvenirs upon the beach.

Beyond that fluid handshake foreign ships roll softly
in the channel, their radios tuned to longwave stations

crackling through the night, songs from Helsinki,
    Tangiers,
or if the fieldfares' wind is right, balalaika drones

from Moscow halls, even Mongol drums – as close as we
    can tell
to the ancient pulse that once blew here from Humber
    on the hill.

Five Minute Nocturne

'Tis the middle of night by the Castle Clock'
—Samuel Taylor Coleridge, 'Christabel'

We were up singing songs round the fire,
drinking wine and setting the world to rights
under the domino night;

your glowing face, my tired body
and our dark silhouettes outlined
by the gadgetry of bats.

The moon hung snug in the crown
of the oak, where a night owl practiced
her one-and-only call in soft iambics.

Across the fields a percussive hound
tested the limits of his lungs and farm
from his kennel in a distant barn.

A lizard sent some pebbles scattering.
The darkness played us out in sculpted sound.
When our voices ceased their chattering
we heard the creatures dreaming underground.

Estuary Music

The quivering call of a curlew
spins from the crescent of its beak.

Wind rings the glockenspiel
of halyards slapping masts

on dry yachts in the boatyard
where a man whistles and sands.

Oystercatchers rise piping
like fifes in a military band.

A raft of tufted ducks dop
together then bounce back up.

Old men strolling old dogs pause
to reprise old conversations –

a mantra of weather forecasts,
a chant of cricket scores.

Two kayaks paddle-smack side to side,
gauging the shrinking channel.

Walkers crunch down grit and shingle,
mussel shells in mud click softly shut.

And the gulls, always the gulls,
yelling their insatiable hunger.

All of this sporadic, improvised
noise doesn't sound like music,

not from this close. Further away
the harmonics resonate,

the maestro's circular breathing
drawing in and releasing the sea,

the birds, boats and old boys
chorusing from cacophony.

Sestina for a Wider Music

Today a moment of epiphany
like falling headlong down a flight of steps
announced itself all glorious and bruised.
Should we redefine what we call 'music' –
reconsider how we categorise
and file it in the index of our minds?

In the garden the sound of birds reminds
me – as I strum upon my Epiphone
electric – it's wrong to categorise
this art as one path walked by human steps
alone. But that's nothing new – the music
of hedgerow birds leaves great composers bruised.

No, there's more to this than the timbre used
by joyous larks trilling out of their minds
at dawn. Think as well of stranger music:
a hatching egg's fanfared epiphany,
the waves surfing down a millipede's step:
there's so much music uncategorised.

Abstract sounds – tyres pummelling cats' glass eyes
on a country road, purple tarmac bruised
by drumming weather, the unceasing step
of storm to sun, the pulse of beetle minds.
Each tide's exodus: an epiphany
of scrubbed shingle – the shoreline's bright music.

Trees groan at a seismic rate, their music
unknown to our ears, just categorised
as susurrus: the fencing wind's epee
fanning through the foiled and gilt-edged leaves, bruised
by Autumn's gales. Such music out of mind,
to us, remote as winds on Russian steppes.

These sounds all have internal rhythmic steps
some so complex we don't hear the music
or comprehend it with our untrained minds.
We're inclined to manmade categories
and other concepts leave our egos bruised.
The Earth's wide song is Man's epiphany.

The Wood Conductor

There was no sign of a woodcutter
in the tin shack raised out of ochre earth
and black wood from an archived forest.
Dismembered trees haunted the air,
ghosts in the pungency of cut pine.

A tepid cup sat by a soiled plate
and a radio murmured, low music
both there and not, a particle of time.
The businessman walked on rutted mulch:
sawdust, wood chips, a chainsaw's rainbow.

A stacked fist of trunks lay seasoning,
patient for the weather to do its work,
sap congealing, slow as a slug's thought.
Under a tarp shelter, a wheel of teeth
stood idle by a pyramid of logs.

A robin hopped and sang, leading him
to the buzz-cut limit of the yard
where chestnuts murmured their faith
in the promise of approaching summer
and two magpies rattled like maracas.

His black Oxfords were crusted with mud
and a spurt of the timber-yard's filth
wrote a warning up his pin-striped leg:
Leave. Leave now!
He loosened his tie, removed his jacket,

rolled his thick shoulders as if wriggling
from a chrysalis, detaching his spine.
The robin was still singing loudly,
music not written in ink on a stave,
but in the helix of the bird's DNA.

Stepping onto a flat-topped stump
with a thin wand he began conducting
the sounds, a fugue concealed in the tune
from the cutter's radio, the bird's song,
all the wild woodwind of the forest.

Shifting Baseline Syndrome

The process by which our perception of the 'natural' world
becomes degraded as the baseline of what is 'natural'
shifts with each new generation.

for Peter Fiennes

When you said 'Shifting Baselines' I believed
you were paying deference to those
hard bop inventions of Charlie Mingus,

Ron Carter's steady licks alongside Miles,
or Jimmy Garrison's pulsating sound
on John Coltrane's sublime *A Love Supreme*,

but you were talking about how, today,
'natural' would be seen by those before us
as 'spoiled', and what *we* see as 'neglected'
our children will soon see as 'natural'...

the way that the sound of the A38
at the end of the garden has replaced
the ambience of birds, with countless tyres
thrumming their hungry pulse against the pitch.

The End of New Orleans

The hump-backed moon walks the late waitress home,
stalks through south-facing yards and dog-piss lawns.

Jazz tourists weave like liquid cadenzas. A cat-house keeper,
crowned with the last bird's nest in town, smokes a 3am reefer.

Pulling at stanchions and wharf-side pilings, the ocean will one day fling
the whole city piecemeal, big and easy, into the end of all things.

It'll take what Katrina left: cars and canes and shotgun shacks.
This time even wealthy white folk floating off in Cadillacs.

A B-flat Selmer plays 'Taps' for the death of the Crescent City,
punching the air downstream where rust gnaws the Chalmette refinery.

The Earth, like some Southern dowager, is tired of silly kids.
Their hideous noise! Their awful mess! Whose are these brats? Get rid!

Her gibbous cousin once lit the lost beasts of prehistory,
great leviathans split his face, a white hubcap on the sea.

The Resolution Quartet in St. Michael's Church

for Marcus Vergette

Bebop made you master of the makeshift stage
while *we* froze on St. Michael's pews:
a throng of faces raising our gaze
to you and the band as you swung your way
through *Skylark* and *Lush Life.*

Rather than resolution, your patter flouted
ironies and risks for Church:
'Here's another song 'bout booze 'n drugs...'
then Charlie sparked a climbing riff,
his puffed and reddened cheeks
issuing a stream of breath as though he was
an angel descending from on high,
with hosts of kooky cherubim & seraphim
to dance some crazy jive before the rood screen.

By *Better Git Hit in Your Soul*
we were so deeply lost in the Blues,
the scrollwork on your bass seemed to fuse
with the church's holy finery,
so rood screen, stage, player and bass
became one united speaker,
as the soft lights chimed from your brass keys and strings
making it possible we could almost believe

you were the Archangel himself,
bearing forth the Holy Banner
with *Giant Steps,* spreading the word.

Take 5 at Ally Pally

The King of the Blues
...Mr B B King!
then Muddy Waters,
Fats Domino too
and the self-proclaimed
originator
of true rock and roll
ol' duckwalking Chuck.
One warm afternoon
in North London sun
lying on trodden
grass with tins of beer,
my future deferred.
All the stars were there:
Stephane Grappelli,
Dizzy Gillespie,
Geordie Alan Price
little Georgie Fame;
I still remember
nearly all the names
– and also that tune
with the extra beat
Dave Brubeck's 'Take Five' –
piano vamping
under Jerry's sax.
Then Lionel Hampton
and his ice-cool vibes...

I'll take that line-up
over any gig
I've attended since.
At Ally Pally
one sweet afternoon
in Seventy-Nine.

Someone To Watch Over Me

Chet Baker, I often think of you
magicking desire from the mouthpiece
of your horn, decked in new
slacks and a striped polo shirt,
hair parted, combed and greased
and *that voice*! lifting us from the dirt...

and also in that hotel room in Amsterdam
leaning on the rails of the balcony
smoking a last-minute cigarette –
your looks shot away and that sweet
voice struggling to hit the harmony –
before the fall... after the final jam.

When Wynton Marsalis Said

Wynton Marsalis at the BBC Proms, Albert Hall, 1993.
The poem ends with the title of Marsalis's suite.

...start low, go very slow; climb higher, catch on fire,
like he was some minister preaching a sermon,

we didn't know the gift that we were in for,
but he puckered up his famous embouchure –

as if he were an angel up in heaven,
or Buddy Bolden down in New Orleans

bringing the marching band back into church –
and channelled everything the crowd was feeling

through the valves and mouthpiece of his cornet.
Beside him, 'Pinecone' Gordon stood sliding

our tension and release from his trombone,
as the septet swung on in painted sound

and we all clapped along in seven-four
to settle *In the Sweet Embrace of Life.*

Synaesthesia

for Jenn Zed

The open window let in the thump and click of hockey
sticks and laced above it the faltering tones of student
clarinet and saxophone as she wrote repeatedly of the
quick brown fox and the lazy dog. 'Dear Sir/Madam...' she
began again on correspondence that'd never see a stamp,
and still her characters leant this way and that in hideous
malformations of the alphabet. At home she scribbled
coloured crayons illustrating sounds she'd heard, the bird
song, hockey clouts, saxophone barks. And now she's paid
to sit in darkened clubs with manga pencils from Japan, as
music pours in lines and scrawls, a racing trace of melody,
a spectrum for sonority, describing chaos in shape and
shade. Still when she signs her work no one can truly read
her name, seeing only a quizzical mark like a hockey stick
the colour of bird song through an open window frame.

Laying Down the Tracks

'Play it again from the top,' said Paul and we shook the last ten versions from our fingers, the way you wring hard labour from your hands. Mine were aching, callused from the *Gibson's* rasping strings and I was losing sight and sound of what it was we were trying to record, like a vanishing figure trudging up and over a hilltop, out of view and earshot, sitting in a disused quarry just beyond the peak to rest his legs and relish in the view, drinking from a flask of warming liquor. Paul rattled the snare and passed a can of beer. 'Take a pull on that for inspiration,' he said and soon we were off again, count-in, drum clicks, first verse, chorus, and then that heart breaking turn to the bridge in all its minor chorded modal glory.

Up on the hilltop the walker raised himself and nodded in the right direction, heading down the steady slope for home...

Suite: Finger Exercises

Left Hand

I. Piano Prelude

after Van Gogh's painting of Marguerite Gachet at the piano

Marguerite collects herself
on the plush velvet stool
in her white cotton dress
under absinthe green walls
whose polka dots spin
like a wheatfield of poppies
in *Auvers-sur-Oise,*
her beehive piled high

as her rudimentary fingers start to sketch
melodies and chords of clotted paint.

2. Saxophone Section

When he walked from that plane crash aged eighty,
Geoff had to lead the village brass-section
from his dining room chair. 'I guess you'll play
second alto saxophone...' he reckoned,

setting me down between the old boys: James
on bass clarinet, Benji on tenor,
and a beard on baritone whose name
I can't recall. Geoff's legs were injured

beyond repair but, man! his fingers
moved faster than mine at thirty-six,
and his ears were acuter and keener,
picking out my bum notes in the mix...

'Having trouble reading the fly shit, boy?'
he'd say, tapping on my hand-written score.

3. Radio Interlude

My mother would listen to Radio 2
while baking a cake in her kitchen.
Upstairs my punk platters span and spat
anarchic curses on the system:
I. Just. Don't. Care.

I'm sure my younger self would want to say
that I've 'sold out' as I sit down to lick
your chocolate cake mix from my fingers
while listening to Country but, honestly, baby,
I. Really. Just. Don't. Care.

4. What the Country Singer Told Me

That the road was not the thing that got her going,
but going that gave her the road.

That if it wasn't for loving the people she liked,
the people she liked might have loved *her*.

That she never saw a man as the freedom to choose,
but the choice to be free of his ways –

it wasn't so much her finger that wore his ring,
as his ring that wore down her finger.

5. Guitar Shop

Browsing all those axes with my son,
lost in his finger-work on fretboards,

I realise how much he's learned alone
and, in the moment's wonder, lose my words.

Right Hand

6. Improvisation

Fingers find their own way,
not moved knowingly –
but as servants
of an external spirit.
The players *will* the music,
yet much less than that –
without conscious thought
they paint the airwaves,
open the dam
to let the river run where it must.
　　How?
An understanding,
a knowledge gained, honed
and laid like keystones
beneath the edifice of music,
supporting but unseen.
Just as you do not think
to move your tongue
to roll it, press it,
to form your words.
You simply speak.

7. Tea with Mingus (in 9/8)

You made the tea,
offered ginger cake
from the Village.
I opened my case,
dusted off strings,
found my finger picks,
took the tea things
into the dry yard.
We played standards
in the hi-rise sun
over your flat.
When I got back home
I found I'd left
my old pork pie hat.

8. The Wide Span

But me?
I'm her old piano teacher –
my hair is white (what's left of it),
my bank account has fewer notes
than Cage's infamous joke.
I've little to show for a life
of grade exams and counting bars.
Still, when I see her slim fingers
move glissando over the keys,
or she trills some fast Scarlatti;
pedals the bass through a Bach fugue
while I wait to turn her pages,
I can't help but note the softness
of her neck, that mole on her jaw,
her salon-styled hair cascading
free as a Kreisler cadenza,
the gleam of her engagement ring...
Then there's an old lock that rattles
and I can hear her duetting
with a dark young man
whose broad hand-span
could rival Liszt's famous reach.
Hands that stretched a full thirteenth
now buckled with arthritis
and the tracing of dotted lines
along all my allotted scores.

9. Amati

she so
resembled
a cello with
her suntanned
back and long dark
plait hanging
down
like a
fingerboard
that he fancied
the notion of tattooing
f holes to either side of
her fine waist. He would put
a bow in her hair and
gently seat her
on a
s
p
i
k
e

10. Two Fingers of Whiskey

Like a young Tom Waits, he leant against the bar
and knocked back two fingers of whiskey
losing himself in the barmaid's kohl-rimmed eyes
and the melancholic music of her humming.

She huffed on the glassware and shone it
with nonchalant swipes of her dishcloth,
polishing his loneliness. How he ached
to switch stools with the pianist on stage,

looking for her sadness and finding it
in the silences between the songs...
those pauses held him mesmerised until
the world came flooding back in glugs of rye:

was that the ice cubes cracking in his glass,
or just her fingers closing round his heart?

Aquifer

Tonight the wind constructs a wasteland
from the garden, unhooking the trees.
Rain spears nickel-bright in the porch light.
I've chased the plastic blow-aways
ripped from the green recycling box
and now, lights off in the quiet kitchen,
I look out at the south-westerly
hauling the Atlantic by its vapours.
How far has this deluge travelled?
From the deep mid-ocean fish tank,
or further, the cold eastern seaboard
where the sullen Hudson passes
the electric towers of my birthplace?
I pour bourbon and search for music
suited to this black and blustery hour.
But what sounds do you turn to
when the night has you unsettled,
like a surge lifting a seated pebble?
'Vigilante Man' with Ry's plaintive slide:
rainy nights down in the engine house?
Or something closer to home: a girl
fluting a ballad of moorland gypsies
itinerant and raggled on the heath?
No, neither of those... I uncase my guitar
and draw from my own inclemency,
a still, dark aquifer below parched earth.

The Audition

'Sing us something, please,' he said, 'if you're going to be our singer,' and she stood on the stage in the spotlight, corpsed, the way that an instruction to party is no basis for a party at all. The faces in the row of seats below her stared up blankly, like a school of koi carp rising in a pond to take some food from the surface, their eyes bulging, their mouths wide open. She opened her own mouth and felt the first breath rising in her windpipe, over the tongue, her lips forming the shape of a word she wasn't sure she knew, nor which would follow closely on its heels... *Where does song come from? From birdsong, stone-age flutes, the singing apes?* The spotlights burned, the stage warmed up, she felt her phrases drawing to a close.

Below her, on the seats, the director's eyes were closed, his face restful. The singer's breath hung on her lips and faded slowly out into the gods

Birdsong

She *sashayed* –
that's the word.
Arrogant, unafraid,
like some fancy water bird,
all beak and breast,
cadences and trills.
Said she sang her best
for hundred-dollar bills –
before shrinking my skin
with a coil of smoke
and something akin
to a lash bat of hope.
Ah, fools just hang themselves:
she simply sold the rope...
But, oh, that lark could sing
and I'd swear an oath
to the God of Ornithology
to see some pink dawn
sneakin' in on me
lying under her downy
flamingo morning
wing.

Riding with Cole Porter

In 1937 the songwriter Cole Porter was crushed by his
falling horse, leaving his legs crippled. He refused
amputation, but his right leg was replaced in 1958 after
countless operations.

Cole Porter, sometimes I think I feel you
riding beside me on horseback
as I sing my way along a country lane,
the hooves of our horses percussing the tarmac
and the hedges bursting with voices of birds.

Perhaps we are sharing the evening air
from the back of our mounts, Cole Porter,
passing time in lazy chat of composition
and the joys of a well-turned lyric, as you
spur into a trot, then kick into canter.

I think of you also, Cole Porter,
in your tailored gabardine, after riding,
your polka dot tie, buttons and cuff links,
hair slicked back and black with Brilliantine,
confident and louche on the photographer's couch.

And then I think of you again, Cole Porter,
underneath your horse's weight,
as you lie in the mud with your legs
crushed flat by the falling hooves... the years
of pain to come, the countless operations

and how you struggled to write through them,
your best songs behind you and the fear
that one may never write a lyric to match.
Maybe *It was just one of those things*, Cole Porter,
before the deferred amputation, the prosthetic limb.

Oh Cole Porter! To ride out with you
one more time, becoming one with the rhythm
of our horses, setting our ears to the wind,
and finding out just where the animal ends
and where the songful human being begins.

On Buying a Horse

Pack a pack horse and rest up here on
Black Country Rock'
    —David Bowie, 'Black Country Rock'

We drove across the moor to view
a mare with David Bowie eyes –
one brown, one blue; one shocked in ice,
the other earth – her skewbald coat
in tan and white a painted map
of the new land we were moving into...
    and all the skylarks of Dartmoor
    were pinned up in the chalk blue air.

When you rode her off across the distant brow
and disappeared, I was left alone,
just me and a herd of highland cows
who stood and lowed dewlap-deep
in a moorland pool, their horns spread wide
as if in supplication to the skies...
    and all the skylarks of Dartmoor
    rang like diamonds in the chalk blue air.

Far off, across the cordoned range,
the army put their bulls' eyes to the test –
the loud retorts of attack, defence,
the heavy thud of shell-fall blending
with the drum beat of our new mount's hooves
as you rode down the dark slope to join me...
    and the whole risen choir of the moor
      were ringing changes in the chalk blue air.

Abraxas

Struck still by the frosted morning
two ponies stand Trojan, waiting

to be inhabited by Abraxas
the dawn bringer, spirit of horse.

In my earbuds *Samba Pa Ti* rises
as chilled air shivers into life.

The magic woman of my teenage dreams
comes to me wild, naked and wilful.

Unstoppable percussion, overdriven guitar.
Such music! *Singing winds, Crying beasts.*

My head has been turned so many times –
spun by a sound, a song, an instrument.

And different artists have carried me,
a rider jumping from steed to steed.

Now, nearing the top of the hill, I look back
at my thousand ponies running in sunlight.

Cabrillo Highway

Crossing the San Mateo County line
between the controlled landscape of my life
and a world of impossibilities
waiting to be tried,
                                     I drop the windows,
crank the volume and Peter Rowan and I
sing full tilt of The Free Mexican Airforce–
Mescalito riding his white horse –
and all the enclosed, rabbity pastures
and ten pub market towns of my homeland
fade, small as the specks of turkey buzzards
floating over dry Californian hills,
and the band of gulls I passed soloing
round Pigeon Point lighthouse, like Bill Monroe's
Bluegrass Boys circling a single mic.

Trout Mask Replica

'A squid eating dough in a polyethylene bag
is fast and bulbous. Got me?'
  —**Captain Beefheart, Trout Mask Replica**

i.m. Iain Potts

Dave gifted you the disks at twenty-one,
Happy Birthday Mate, emblazoned on
their inner sleeves in psychedelic patterns.
The three of us would sit and listen, lost
in contrapuntal dissonance, enchanted
by Drumbo's polyrhythmic clattering,
Zoot Horn Rollo's floating glass finger and
The Captain's cacophonous clarinet.

When the gatefold finally came to me
I can't recall, but you had upped and gone
to New York City, while the vinyl stayed
in my collection.   By fifty you were dead –
fast and bulbous – your disks spinning on my deck.
When he turned eighteen, I gave them to my son.

Decades

The 80s were comfortable, weren't they?
like a new pair of Sta-Prest and loafers,
a button-down collar and cheap Harrington
bought down the market for a song.
We were dancing to *The Specials*,
Dandy Livingstone, Toots and the Maytals,
working our elbows like pistons oiled
by cheap tins of lager. When they stumbled in
the 90s were comfortably numb, spaced out
and lounging on the sofa to retro –
the 70s still had us in their grip –
though no one was dancing to Dylan,
least of all Dylan himself. The Noughties?
no memory of them at all. Bland boy bands,
girl pop, the whole clubbing thing,
while the only dance we were doing
was the Up-and-Downstairs at midnight
to the box room underneath the roof,
the crying of babies, sterilised bottles of milk
and the soothing drip of *Tixylix* and *Calpol*
that wrote our tune and metronomed our time.

The Blue Guitarist

I know my lazy, leaden twang
Is like the reason in a storm;

And yet it brings the storm to bear.
I twang it out and leave it there.
     —Wallace Stevens, 'The Man With the Blue Guitar'

The blue man with the Dobro on his lap
is disenchanted with his sliding licks –
they refuse to climb the fluid staircase
of their dreaming so nimbly any more
and seem to hang instead upon the frets
like sleepwalkers hindered by each footfall.

When they *do* reach the summit, they snooze
on cushions under drapes, like runaway
children hiding from each other in a game
to fill a rainy afternoon... as when we were kids
and climbed the narrow steps up to the loft
where the playroom hunkered underneath the eaves

and there we watched the notes of rain describe
the glass and the late afternoon sunshine
and thought of our tomcat who disappeared
and turned-up dead in a neighbour's outhouse,
curled inside a crate for storing apples
like an old guitar secure within its case.

The Luthier's Love Song

Although you have just the *five* fingers,
  I built her as a test with these *six* strings.
    Hold her to you as you would your other
    half, under your arm and close to your chest.
  Sense her murmur through your ribcage –
the resonance of an improvised love.

    Her headstock is the prow of a sound ship,
  her song the warm echo of maple and spruce
and the whiplash-down-the-rails of coiled bronze wire.
That screech of tortoiseshell along the strings
  is the sound that you hear as love breaks – feel it
    linger in her ripened patina of wood.

Elegy for Chris

i.m. Chris Ayliffe

Cutting yew, Chris left the back door open,
until the rain came squalling from the east.
Rinky-tink banjos hung on nicotine walls
with butterfly bowl-backs and hybrid beasts.

We stood beside the dusty work bench
on a mat of Sid-the-Lurcher's hair,
a wood-shaving and sawdust sweetness;
the scent of flame and birds-eye in the air.

Guitars were fettled – but we mostly drank
while he told sixties' myths and stories:
Ralph's parrot from a Luton taxi rank;
Bert's booze, Davey's madness, Renbourn's furies.

Then we contemplated the big Tamworth
he'd named – so couldn't send for joints and chops,
corralling it up and down a muddy field
until it fell, a dead weight, in the slop.

The way things go I wasn't there that day,
or many times again before Chris died.
I heard they buried the dead pig where it lay
and someone said they saw the old boy cry.

My Grandpa's Banjulele

He passed it on to me at my sixteenth –
no flying V, or Telecaster,
no Shadows Strat, or Les Paul rocker –
more a hangover from the war

when Formby wore his suit and dickie
and strummed his Gibson ukulele
Leaning on a Lamppost... those catgut strings,
the hardwood body inlaid with nacre

round the drum, a wooden bridge to resonate
and the greasy lustre of generations
walking up and down the fingerboard
to the maker's branded headstock: *Keech*.

I learned the basic songbook chords,
their mixture of ratchet and melody
calling the Variety Hall back to life,
the barbershop quartet, the one-man band.

Now it hangs on the sitting room wall,
its drum skin split, the bridge mislaid.
I bring it out at socials, stroke the teak,
try to recall the timbre of its voice.

Treasure Hunting

Her name, if I had ever spoken it, would have been floral and dusty on the tongue, dry in the throat – as if *Chintz* could be a name. Her skirts were curtains across a stage long closed and, as she shuffled between stacks of clutter, anyone could see she was the living spirit of salvage. A simple accountant of surplus stock from other peoples' yesterdays. Surely someone must want something from her crowded shelves and phantom-filled parlours? Always these disused chapels and back-street brick-a-brac stores were cold, a gas heater sweating near a desk and kettle. Once I hunted through them for lost treasures: mandolins from before the Great War, when the golden age of eight-string orchestras was in full pluck. Such house clearance stores are gone now, lost to the internet where nothing is allowed to be hidden for true seekers of the obscure, where every piece of questionable junk is matched instantly to its global devotee, and every item has a known value. Still, I have this recurrent dream where I'm searching among clumsy wardrobes, worn-shouldered armchairs, wind-up gramophones, ugly vases and cutlery canteens, for a forgotten but perfect Vinaccia: spruce, ebony and rosewood, bone headstock finial; or better, behind a walnut chest I open a black coffin case to expose a Luigi Embergher 5 bis, fluted maple ribs shining like pirate gold under the gaze of the shopkeeper, floating by, blousy as a figurehead.

A Ghost Speaks of Music

There was once so little human music
in this world. Before your radios blared.
Fidgeting choirs in parish churches,
the scraping fiddle at a country fair.

An organ grinder in his tattered hat
or, exalted above the common man,
baroque recitals to powdered wigs
in mansions overlooking sculpted land.

But for farm folk living up muddy lanes
the daily music which we mostly knew
came from penny broadsheet balladeers
and the plainsong bleat of lamb and ewe.

Not like *you* with your streaming and your phones
surrounded constantly by man-made sound,
strangers to the sanctity of silence.
Music to you is something cheaply found

and soon discarded, not the precious art
or joyful reel we'd walk ten miles to hear
and ten miles back again, humming over
until we had it memorised by ear.

Then next day, after stabling the horses,
our Bill would lean his back against the wall
and sing the new song, his voice a cannon
in the yard they could hear up at the hall.

I swear his baritone could shatter stone
and though he's gone a century and more,
you drop a hammer in the yard – he'll sing
its pitch at you across the flagstone floor.

There are ghosts in an old song's melody
Early in the morning on a day so bright and new...
and we call to you through the bars of time
...we come to scythe the tall grass as reaper-men must do.

The Old Joanna

After work my grandpa tuned pianos,
although he had no music in his bones
and owned a pedal-driven pianola.
But his pitch was true and he knew his trade.

My father played a kitsch electric organ
with stops and pedals – his arpeggios,
celeste and special presets echoed through
the 80s, like a score by Philip Glass.

From principle he wouldn't play piano:
'You couldn't give the things away back then,'
he said, 'so people used to smash them up
when they wanted shot of their Joanna.'

Both are gone, yet both remain, as I tune in
through the wall to my neighbour's muffled scales.

One Man Band

'Perhaps I may become a highwayman again
Or I may simply be a single drop of rain
But I will remain
And I'll be back again and again and again...'
—Jimmy Webb, 'The Highwayman'

Once I was an old harmonium
rattling out mantras and mesmeric drones
from a hardwood box. My leather
bellows breathed the desert's heat.

Then I was a saxophone: a 1930s
silver horn. My susurrating reed and bell
filled spaces in the back row of the band
from where I beckoned down the yearning night.

There came a time I was a clarinet:
all dark wood and mercury tears.
Other nights I was percussion – djembe
and a neem wood cable drum from Kathmandu.

I have been *Telecaster*, *Takamine*;
and theremin, an upright piano
the kids thumped, then learned
to embrace with finesse.

I have been violin, and violin bass –
the backing band section of eddies and footfall.
Once or twice I've even played the soloist.
And I'll come back,
                    reprise,
                              I will return...

The Day Elvis Died

The ferry must have sailed throughout the night
since you were in pyjamas at the bar
watching the news as you cruised back from France,
the family vacation at a close.

Waves tossed the vessel, gently at first
and then becoming rougher with the storm.
What *was* that all the adults were discussing?
Who was *The King* and what on earth were *Quaaludes*?

How quickly everything is forgotten:
what you did and said, the places you stayed,
the name of that *jeune fille* with whom you played.
Triumphs. Childhood. Fame... and its addictions.

Forty years on in a game of charades,
your stepson's never even *heard* of him.

'A Dead Soldier Jigged in the Small-Town Square'

i.m. Edward Thomas

A dead soldier jigged in the small-town square
while people walked by – most blind to his dance.
He had more wounds than a sad heart could bear.

He scattered wild flowers all through the air,
but the crowds milled past avoiding his glance,
that soldier who jigged in the small-town square.

He dressed in bunting from the Easter fair;
the town's people looked afraid and askance.
He had more wounds than a sad heart could bear.

He remembered and sang folk songs and airs –
the lost tunes of England whistled through France –
that soldier who jigged in the small-town square.

His thin face was white, frost tinselled his hair,
the road he'd taken was chosen by chance.
He had more wounds than a sad heart could bear.

He's gone again now, and I can't say where,
perhaps he's lost in bucolic romance,
that soldier who jigged in the small-town square:
he had more wounds than a sad heart could bear.

At *Beaumont Hamel*

'It's a god-awful small affair...'
—*David Bowie*

We made a summer tour across the Somme,
discovering those villages to which
platoons of boys were sent from Norfolk camps,
camps your great-aunt called on in the war –
she, the baker's girl, delivering bread
to thin squaddies from the back of the cart,
swapping her batches of warm white loaves
for farewell signatures of future ghosts.

A lyric from a song had us ear-wormed
as we drove around the trenches, unable
to place it... *from Ibiza to the Norfolk Broads.*
'Call Paul,' you said. I phoned. 'That's *Life on Mars.*'
I cursed him, then thanked him, feeling the dead
press at our windows from their unmarked graves.

Elegy for Carl

i.m. Carl Hamer

Last night I saw you again,
playing music in a garden
neither of us ever knew,
below fruit trees strung with candle lights.
It was an early evening in late September.
You strummed and sang
...I must've been through 'bout a thousand girls...
while I noodled and harmonised
...fooled around and fell in love...
Afterwards you cracked some innuendo,
and we laughed like the teenagers
we hadn't been for many years.

Helen had gone inside to check the roast chicken
and when the next song finished you stood up,
lit a cigarette and slid away coughing.

Winter was suddenly somewhere close,
so I gathered my plectrums
knowing I wouldn't find them after dark,
propped your old Radiotone guitar
against a white garden chair
and walked under the low apple boughs
towards the house.

The lights were off and silence
drifted out like a great eraser.
                    I made my exit
through the side gate, pursued by bare
morning, cold birdsong,
and a dwindling band of troubadours.

But, ah, the smell of that chicken cooking,
the dinner we might one day have
...*I loved 'em and I left 'em alone...*

Lark Ascending

No one knew for sure where *Whistling Steve*
disappeared to – one day he was present
digging holes in the road for electrics,
sewage pipes and cables. Then he wasn't.

A day at work could not be called complete
without a stream of unremitting trills
escaping on his breath; without the piercing
klaxon of his catcall as a girl passed by;
without his army riffs, his lark ascending.

When drains and gullies needed clearing
Whistling Steve was there, his shovel shouldered,
his lips alive with melody. But when
the world went wireless he simply dissolved,
like birdsong fading in a rising wind.

Wild Rufus

after Elmore James 'The Sky is Crying'

Wild Rufus played sax in the Duke of York
jamming with Deano in the old tap room.
Mostly twelve bars: Muddy Waters, Son House,
Elmore James – *I believe I'll dust my broom.*

I snuck in late with my underage mates
trying our best to look bigger and older.
The bar was full of fairytale giants –
the biker landlord: a B.S.A. ogre.

The mind-swirling stink of Black Moroccan,
wet wool, leather, British motorbike grease,
the sense that trouble was a curse away –
a punch up, a blade, the threat of police.

The crowd moved knowingly, Rufus sat down
to play solo in the eye of the bar.
Sunny, yesterday my life was filled with rain...
Without a mic, he bellowed a capella

before blasting wildly through the changes.
He had leaves in his hair and some thin guy
said he lived in a van on the common
and once cut a record with Humble Pie.

Everyone cheered when he finished his turn.
He grinned – teeth like chips from a broken hoof –
shook his big head, shambled up to the bar,
as Deano and the boys resumed their groove.

The landlord called lock-in but I slid away
singing blues to the rhythm of my feet.
Half way home Elmore's sky started to cry –
Oh, look at the tears rolling down the street.

An Old Musician's Love Song

'Let us go then you and I...'
—*T.S. Eliot, 'The Love Song of J. Alfred Prufrock'*

I hear there is a chance you'll be
somewhere in the near vicinity
sometime soon, or at least before too long –
so, if you are, perhaps you'll look me up
and come around for supper
and a song?
And, if not, then no matter,
it is, after all, years since we have had a natter
and, when all that's said and done reaches its ends,
what's a few more years of silence between friends?

It's simply that I miss the cool and clear
strokes of your conversation,
just as, come winter, I miss that time of year
when carefree-ness and sunshine sweep the nation.
Mine is the moment's distemperate weather.
I am an improvised man. A performer.
I am blessed with the basic equipment of thinking,
of playing tunes and getting by,
no problem. Like a boy with a fly
in a bottle
I am happy in and with myself. At least a little.
And when I'm not, well, there's always drinking.

Yet every so often I hear your voice from afar,
like the faint scrape of a plectrum on the strings of a
guitar
and I weep, or nearly come to weeping.
In the yard it will soon be time for sweeping
the leaves and piling them ready to burn.
Then it will be time for us to turn
in for the winter
and wait for the stark news of the season's printer –
these black marks on our personal snow.

And then it will be time for me to go –
me, my body; me, myself –
shuffling round my quarters
for small answers
to big questions
kept in place by the grave shelf
that slips away like the ocean's.

Until then it's still the same routine:
the why, the wherefore, the what-might-have-been.
So, if you're near, why not, indeed, drop by?
We can sit up late and mend the world with song,
and put by old bygones,
you and I.

Grace Notes

Seeking a pulse the doctor lifts her hand
and finds himself connected to her beat,
unsteady now, arrhythmic in repeat,
but once as constant as a marching band,
insistent as carnival timbale,
the rhythm of her life a simple groove
scored by the way in which the heavens move:
the circling of worlds, of night and day.

Over this her melody lay threaded
like strings and swags of party lights along
the stave of time. Love, marriage, family,
the usual constancies of a wedded
life, some grace notes embellishing the song:
a kiss, a lie, a stab of poetry.

Tinnitus

Sometimes I hope the ringing din
might carry hidden words within

> *the quiet closing of an unoiled door;*
> *the restless squeaking of a garden gate,*

but I hear nothing in the roar
no matter how I concentrate.

> *the rush of urgent rivers on the moor;*
> *a taxi idling when the hour is late.*

So now I seek external noise,
to overcome the steady gale

> *Long driven waves collapsing without choice,*
> *which churn and grind the rock-fall into shale;*

that doesn't bring your gentle voice,
but only thoughts of where I failed

> *the distant droning of an LA plane;*
> *a kettle coming to the boil again.*

The Music Lesson

When I came down to the kitchen for breakfast
Music was already awake, turning up the radio
and scanning through white noise and babble
to tune to his favourite station:

'I was there when Butler shouted *Judas!*'
Music bragged, as Dylan's *Like A Rolling Stone*
filled the kitchen with a swirl of organ
and I smiled knowingly, mumbling my way

from verse to refrain. Static fizzed and,
through the haunting choir of tuned-up voices –
newsreaders, adverts, unknown languages –
Music's fingers led us somewhere new:

'No denying it, punk rock changed the way
we think and dress.' I nodded to the Pistols
and looked down at my sheepskin slippers.
'Or maybe you prefer the Blues?' Already

I was ear wormed... *I woke up this morning...*

Song : *Shibboleth*

Shib-bo-leth: **n.** *a common saying or belief*

When Presidents lie through the gaps in their teeth
and what was above is now lying beneath;
when you're anxious for truth and are vexed about death–
    Return to the breath.

When the broadcasts are filled with political whims
and lenses zoom-in upon car bombs and limbs;
when the facts read much more like the plot of Macbeth –
    Return to the breath.

When the world stage is shaken by missiles and storms
and nations surrender to populist norms,
though drugs might appeal, don't go turning to meth –
    Return to the breath.

When *having opinions* presides over proof
and half of the news was made up on the hoof,
you might well attend to the old shibboleth:
    Return to the breath.

Lullaby for Rosie

Lay the night upon you
like a cloak of quiet stars,
wear a honeysuckle garland
carry sunny-garden flowers,
then wander wet-foot with me
to the bank beside the stream
on the grass all dark and dewy,
where the slipping current gleams.
We'll shrink to tiny water fleas,
sail our nutshell boat away
down along the tinfoil river
to the lapping moony bay
where the fish will sing beside us
their libretti of the deep
and we'll rule the sea like pirates
till our parrots go to sleep,
droop and nod
their heavy beaks
then not a word
we'll speak
till warm beneath
    our cloak of stars
        we too
          will
          softly
          fall
        a s l e e p

A Theory of Music

for Kelvin Corcoran

One river evokes every river, they say,
each drop of water summoning all others,

just as each note a singer breathes, conjures
every song that ever left a tongue...

like the night of that concert in Brussels,
enthralled by the Estonian National Choir,

after we sat up for hours at yours
as the night birds called the darkness down

and we cried – and I mean *really cried* –
while Nina broke our sentimental hearts

with *I Know What It Is To Be Free*...
just as I cried when Susan Tedeschi took us

to *Midnight In Harlem* with that deep
liquescent voice of hers and I stood there

with my hands aloft like a convert, sobbing,
while Derek Trucks coaxed his guitar

into a raga riff that had me all the way back
to Jaipur, 1991, and that troupe

of Rajasthani folk players striking up a reel
on harmonium, *dholak*, *alghoza* and *dhadd*

that is pulsing in my dance bones still,
shanti   shanti   shanti

Silence

       creeps calmly over level fields,
     settles like snow in back lane drifts.
It's the armistice where sea and sky yield,
inhalation's pause before breathing shifts.
Carthusian prayer in habit and hood,
a half-forgotten thought closing its eyes.
Emerald ferns bowing in evening woods,
a place where vibration comes to die -
its agitated wave a tightened thread.
The sub-atomic void; guitars unplayed,
a dusty cello leaning. Words unsaid.
An absent coda for the end of days.

ABOUT THE AUTHORS

Andy Brown is Professor of English & Creative Writing at Exeter University and known widely as a distinguished poet and writing tutor. His many poetry books include *Casket* (Shearsman, 2019); *Bloodlines* (Worple, 2018); *Exurbia* (Worple, 2014); *The Fool and the Physician* (Salt, 2012); *Goose Music* (with John Burnside, Salt, 2008) and *Fall of the Rebel Angels: Poems 1996-2006* (Salt, 2006). He co-edited *A Body of Work: an anthology of poetry and medicine* (Bloomsbury, 2016) and edited *The Writing Occurs As Song: a Kelvin Corcoran Reader* (Shearsman, 2015). His study of literary and artistic tree climbing and wellbeing, *The Tree Climbing Cure*, is published by Bloomsbury. He is a singer-songwriter and has recorded and gigged solo and with a number of bands.

Marc Woodward's chapbook *A Fright of Jays* was published by Maquette Press in 2015 and his first full collection, *Hide Songs* by Green Bottle Press in 2018. This was followed in 2020 by his first collaboration with Andy Brown, *The Tin Lodes,* published by Indigo Dreams Press. His second full collection *Shaking the Persimmon Tree* was published by Sea Crow Press in 2022.

He has published poems in a wide variety of magazines, anthologies and websites, and has performed his work regularly. In addition to his writing, he is also a well-respected musician who has performed and taught internationally. His album *Bluemando* is available on iTunes and Spotify.

ABOUT THE PRESS

Sea Crow Press is an independent publisher committed to amplifying voices. In a rapidly changing world, we believe the small press plays an essential part in contemporary arts as a community forum, a cultural reservoir, and an agent of change. We are international with a focus on our New England roots. We publish creative nonfiction, fiction, and poetry and our books celebrate our connection to each other and to the natural world with a focus on positive change and great storytelling. We have been building a literary community since 2020.

LINER NOTES

(FOR THE INSISTENTLY CURIOUS)

Marc:

lead voc., mandolin, rain stick and shaker on tracks no.

1, 4, 5, 7, 8, 9, 11, 13, 14, 15, 17, 19, 22, 25, 27, 30, 31,
36, 38, 39, 43, 45, 47, 49, 50, 53, 55
and nos. 6, 7, 8 and 9 of the Finger Exercises suite.

Andy:

lead voc., guitar, bass, saxophone on tracks no.

2, 3, 6, 10, 12, 16, 18, 20, 21, 23, 26, 28, 29, 32, 33, 34, 35, 37,
40, 41, 42, 44, 46, 48, 51, 52, 54,
and nos.1, 2, 3, 4, 5 and 10 of the Finger Exercises suite.

Harmonies throughout by both.

CPSIA information can be obtained
at www.ICGtesting.com
Printed in the USA
BVHW080242270123
657224BV00003B/60